A **TRUE** BOOK™

National Parks
Glacier

JOANNE MATTERN

Children's Press®
An Imprint of Scholastic Inc.

Content Consultant
James Gramann, PhD
Professor, Department of Recreation, Park and Tourism Sciences
Texas A&M University, College Station, Texas

Library of Congress Cataloging-in-Publication Data
Names: Mattern, Joanne, 1963– author.
Title: Glacier / by Joanne Mattern.
Description: New York, NY : Children's Press, an imprint of Scholastic Inc., [2018] | Series: A true
 book | Includes bibliographical references and index.
Identifiers: LCCN 2017025793 | ISBN 9780531235065 (library binding) | ISBN 9780531238097 (pbk.)
Subjects: LCSH: Glacier National Park (Mont.)—Juvenile literature. | Natural history—Montana—
 Glacier National Park—Juvenile literature.
Classification: LCC F737.G5 M378 2018 | DDC 978.6/52—dc23
LC record available at https://lccn.loc.gov/2017025793

All rights reserved. Published in 2018 by Children's Press, an imprint of Scholastic Inc.
Printed in Heshan, China 62

SCHOLASTIC, CHILDREN'S PRESS, A TRUE BOOK™, and associated logos are trademarks and/or
registered trademarks of Scholastic Inc.

Scholastic Inc., 557 Broadway, New York, NY 10012

1 2 3 4 5 6 7 8 9 10 R 27 26 25 24 23 22 21 20 19 18

Front cover (main): A meadow of wildflowers
Front cover (inset): A kayaker
on Bowman Lake
Back cover: Red Jammer bus on
Going-to-the-Sun Road

Find the Truth!

Everything you are about to read is true *except* for one of the sentences on this page.

Which one is **TRUE**?

T or F Fur trappers were the first people to see Glacier National Park.

T or F The ice of the park's glaciers can be up to 100 feet (30.5 m) thick.

Find the answers in this book.

In 1932, Waterton Lakes National Park in Canada and Glacier National Park were united to form the Waterton-Glacier International Peace Park.

CHAPTER 1

A Park Formed by Glaciers

Can you imagine a place where huge, icy **glaciers** streak the sides of towering mountain peaks? Can you picture beautiful green forests growing along the shores of huge, blue lakes? That is exactly what you'll find at Glacier National Park in northwest Montana. Whether you like to hike, camp, or just enjoy the scenery from your car window, you will be amazed at the beauty in the park's natural landscape.

Glacier National Park

Going-to-the-Sun Road provides visitors easy access to much of Glacier National Park.

Going-to-the-Sun Road

In the early 1900s, it was difficult for visitors to reach some of the park's most beautiful places by car. But in 1921, workers began building a new road that would make the park much more accessible. Eleven years later, in 1932, Going-to-the-Sun Road opened. The road led through the mountains and across the park. The road has been called one of the most beautiful routes in America. It was named a National Historic **Landmark** in 1997.

National Park Fact File

A national park is land that is protected by the federal government. It is a place of importance to the United States because of its beauty, history, or value to scientists. The U.S. Congress creates a national park by passing a law. Here are some key facts about Glacier National Park.

Glacier National Park	
Location	Montana
Year established	1910
Size	1,012,837 acres (409,881 hectares)
Average number of visitors each year	2.9 million
Tallest mountain	Mount Cleveland at 10,466 feet (3,190 meters)
Deepest lake	Lake McDonald at 464 feet (141 m) deep

Bearhat Mountain rises above Hidden Lake in central Glacier National Park.

CHAPTER 2

The Lay of the Land

From the mountaintops to the valleys below, each part of Glacier National Park's landscape holds different wonders. Almost three million people visit every year to experience the park's wide range of natural beauty. They enjoy lakes, waterfalls, and rushing streams. They can explore fields full of flowers or thick mountain forests. They can even climb the park's rocky mountains to get a view from above.

Different types of wildflowers grow at different elevations in the park.

Animals Big and Small

Because Glacier National Park has such a diverse range of **ecosystems,** it is also home to an amazing range of animals. Tiny insects buzz through the air as huge mammals wander among the trees. The water is packed with fish, and birds of all kinds flit through the air.

There are 29 species of birds of prey in Glacier National Park.

Black bears are North America's most common bear species.

Living Large

Bears are some of the largest animals you'll find in the park. Male grizzly bears can weigh more than 450 pounds (204 kilograms) and be up to 6 feet (2 m) tall. Black bears are smaller than grizzlies, but they can still weigh up to 250 pounds (113 kg). These animals can be very dangerous. Visitors to the park are advised to stay at least 100 yards (91.4 m) away from any bears they see.

Little brown bat

Scientific name: *Myotis lucifugus*

Habitat: Caves and trees

Diet: Insects

Fact: Bats are the only mammals that can fly.

Golden eagle

Scientific name: *Aquila chrysaetos*

Habitat: Mountains and open meadows

Diet: Small mammals, reptiles, birds

Fact: Golden eagles grab their prey with their sharp talons.

Common loon

Scientific name: *Gavia immer*

Habitat: Lakes

Diet: Fish

Fact: Common loons are black and white in the summer, but turn gray and white in the winter.

Western painted turtle

Scientific name: *Chrysemys picta*

Habitat: Ponds, lakes, marshes

Diet: Earthworms, insects, water plants

Fact: During the winter, this turtle hibernates in the mud at the bottoms of lakes or ponds.

CHAPTER 4

The Park's Plants

Glacier National Park is home to an amazing variety of plants growing in different areas. Some plants flourish in the warmer, wetter parts of the park. Others can only grow in the cold mountains. From the cedar and pine forests in the west to the flowers and bushes that grow in the lower elevations, Glacier is packed with plants.

Tall trees provide homes for many mammals, birds, and insects.

East and West

The warmer western part of the park features cedar and hemlock forests. Some of the trees in these forests have been growing for hundreds of years. White spruces and cottonwoods grow at lower elevations. Ferns and moss grow on the damp forest floor.

The eastern part of the park is cooler and drier. The trees here are mostly aspens. Grassy meadows are also a common sight.

High Elevations

Tundra is found in the highest elevations. Here, tiny flowers and lichens grow on the rocks and in the shallow soil. Sturdy evergreens grow at the edge of the **treeline**.

Lichen

Beargrass

Middle Elevations

Spruce and poplar trees grow in the middle elevations. In wetter areas, thick forests of cedar and hemlock are common. Some of these trees are more than 500 years old!

Cedar

Spruce

Low Elevations

At lower elevations, ferns and moss grow on the forest floor, while meadows are filled with grasses and colorful wildflowers. In river valleys, the leaves of aspen trees turn brilliant yellow and orange in the fall.

Ferns

Aspen

The park's worst fire season in history occurred in 2003, when more than 135,000 acres (54,633 ha) of forest burned.

CHAPTER 5

Looking Toward the Future

Like many natural habitats, Glacier National Park faces many different problems. Although the land, plants, and animals are protected by laws, disasters can still harm the park. Some of these disasters are natural, while others are created by humans. For example, Glacier has serious problems with forest fires. Most of these fires are caused by lightning strikes, but some are the result of human carelessness.

Map Mystery

One of the most popular places to stay in the park is near a famous lake. Follow the directions below to find the answer.

Directions

1. Start at the Visitor Center at the eastern edge of the park.

2. Sail southwest along the lake that shares its name with the Visitor Center where you began.

3. Climb over the mountains through the pass, or gap, west of the lake.

4. Head southwest toward the road that was named a National Historic Landmark in 1997.

5. When you reach a large lake, you'll see the lodge where people love to stay.

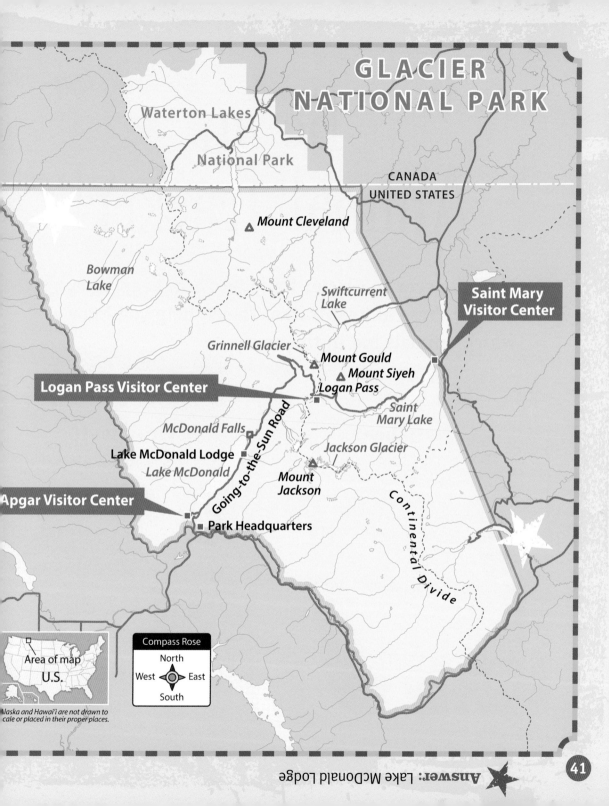

GLACIER
NATIONAL PARK

Waterton Lakes

National Park

CANADA
UNITED STATES

△ Mount Cleveland

Bowman
Lake

Swiftcurrent
Lake

Saint Mary
Visitor Center

Grinnell Glacier

Mount Gould
△ Mount Siyeh
Logan Pass

Logan Pass Visitor Center

Saint
Mary Lake

McDonald Falls

Jackson Glacier

Lake McDonald Lodge

Lake McDonald

Mount
Jackson

Apgar Visitor Center

Going-to-the-Sun Road

Continental Divide

Park Headquarters

Area of map
U.S.

Alaska and Hawai'i are not drawn to
scale or placed in their proper places.

Compass Rose

North

West ◆ East

South

Be an Animal Tracker!

If you're ever in Glacier National Park, keep an eye out for these animal tracks. They'll help you know which animals are in the area.

Grizzly bear
Paw length: 9 to 12 inches (23 to 30.5 centimeters)

Gray wolf
Paw length: 4.5 inches (11.5 cm)

Marmot
Paw length: 3.5 inches (9 cm)

Mountain goat
Hoof length: 3.5 inches (9 cm)

Elk
Hoof length: 5 to 6 inches (12.5 to 15 cm)

Ring-necked pheasant
Foot length: 3 inches (7.5 cm)

Number of glaciers: 25

Number of mountains: 175

Total length of streams inside the park: 2,865 mi. (4,610 km)

Number of waterfalls: 200

Number of lakes: 762

Total length of trails in the park: 746 mi. (1,200 km)

Number of fish species in the park: 24

Number of mammal species: 71

Number of bird species: 276

Did you find the truth?

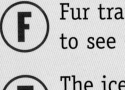

F Fur trappers were the first people to see Glacier National Park.

T The ice of the park's glaciers can be up to 100 feet (30.5 m) thick.

Resources

Books

Flynn, Sarah Wassner, and Julie Beer. *National Parks Guide U.S.A.*
  Washington, DC: National Geographic, 2016.

Graf, Mike. *Glacier National Park: Going to the Sun*. Guilford, CT:
  FalconGuides, 2012.

Stein, R. Conrad. *Montana*. New York: Children's Press, 2015.

**Visit this Scholastic website for more
information on Glacier National Park:**
  ★ www.factsfornow.scholastic.com
  Enter the keyword **Glacier**

About the Author

Joanne Mattern has written more than 250 books for children. She especially likes writing about all the amazing places on our planet. Joanne also loves to write about animals, plants, and the natural world. She grew up in New York State and still lives there with her husband, four children, and several pets.